Sophie Goes to Basketball Camp

Sophie Goes to Basketball Camp

Sarah Fischer Pointer

This book is dedicated to the employees, volunteers, and participants of the Rockford Park District and the Rockford Jr. Chariots for their care and dedication to teamwork and excellence. It is also dedicated to all the University of Illinois at Urbana-Champaign Wheelchair Sports Programs and the annual Wheelchair Basketball Camp for their tireless determination to train and prepare the next generation of wheelchair athletes. Special mention goes out to Mike Frogley and Stephanie Wheeler, who have been leaders in the wheelchair basketball community for many years.

Of course, we can not forget the friends that we've lost along the way. This book is for my fellow Rockford Jr. Chariot, Alex Konitski, aka "Shorty." Your infectious laugh and love for basketball filled all of our hearts, and you will never be forgotten.

Finally, this book is dedicated to the memory of all of those we lost in the COVID 19 pandemic, and, in particular, my loving husband, Darren. I will carry your love in my heart forever. Until I see you again, dear.

1

2

Sophie Swanson had just finished her first year of playing wheelchair basketball. She had learned how to dribble and pass the ball from her chair, and she'd gotten pretty good at it. Now, Sophie wanted to work on her speed so she could keep up with the bigger kids and get better at defense. To help her improve her skills, Sophie's parents surprised her with a basketball chair.

Sophie's new chair was lower to the ground than her regular wheelchair. This meant it could go a lot faster, and the wheels were tilted more than the wheels on her regular chair, making it easier to turn. There was even a bar in front of the chair that she could use to stop another player.

3

When Sophie tried out her new wheelchair for the first time, she felt like she was in a race car! She sped down the court as fast as lightning and stopped quickly at the other end. Sophie was sure she could keep up with anyone in her new chair.

Even though basketball season was over, Sophie was excited for summer because she was going to go to basketball camp for the first time! Every year, the University of Illinois held a wheelchair basketball camp, and Sophie was going this year! She was a little afraid to be away from home for a week, but she was more excited to see her friends again and to play basketball in her new chair.

4

5

6

Camp started on a blazing hot day in June. When her mother pulled their car into the parking lot, Sophie saw there were already a lot of kids who were talking and laughing together. There were also a lot of parents bringing the campers' bags inside and saying their goodbyes.

Sophie found a short, brown-haired woman sitting at a table outside the building near a sign that said, "Illinois Street Residences."

"Name, please?" the woman asked.

"Sophie Swanson."

"Swanson . . . You'll be in Room 108." She handed Sophie a key. "I'm Coach Wellner, and I'll be one of your coaches this week. Welcome to camp!"

"Thank you!"

7

8

Sophie and her mother took her bags inside and looked for her room. When she opened the door, Sophie saw that she had a roommate: it was Ginny! The girls hugged and talked about how excited they were to be at camp.

After giving Sophie a quick hug and kiss, her mom left.

"Isn't this so cool?!" Ginny cried. "And we get to start playing right away! We have practice in an hour."

9

Sophie and Ginny went to the lobby to meet the other campers. A short man in a shiny, silver wheelchair soon came in with some other adults. "Hello! My name is Coach Frawley. I'm the head wheelchair basketball coach here at the U of I, and I'd like to welcome you to camp. I hope you're ready, because your training begins right now. Everyone line up, and we'll head to the gym!"

They finally reached a building called the Activities and Recreation Center, and Coach Frawley called the campers together in the gym. "One of the most important things in wheelchair basketball is speed. You have to be fast enough to keep up with all the other players. I want everyone to line up on the starting line and push as hard as you can to the other end."

10

11

12

The kids lined up on the starting line, and the coaches timed them as they raced down the court. Sophie zipped across the room so fast that she barely noticed she had passed the other starting line!

"Good hustle!" called Coach Wellner. "If you lean forward a little when you push, you can get more strength out of each one."

"Okay, I'll try! Thanks!" Sophie answered.

At afternoon practice, the coaches showed them the first style of playing defense. First, they learned about one-on-one defense.

"This is when one person on defense chooses one player on the other team to guard and stays with them the whole time the other team has the ball," Coach Frawley explained. "Be sure to always call out to your teammates to let them know who you're guarding so they don't have to worry about guarding that person, too."

To show them how it was done, Coach Frawley went up to Coach Wellner and blocked her with his chair. "I've got Wellner!" he cried as he stopped her every move.

The campers practiced one-on-one defense with a partner for a while before the coaches handed out basketballs. The partners then took turns as the player on defense and the player with the ball. Ginny partnered with Sophie, and the two started practicing.

13

With her regular chair, Sophie would have had a hard time keeping up with Ginny. But with her new basketball chair, it was easy. Ginny moved to the right, and Sophie blocked her. Ginny backed up a little, and Sophie stopped her. She was getting good at this!

During their morning practice the next day, Coach Frawley taught the campers about zone defense.

"In zone defense you choose an area of the court to defend. You guard whoever is on the other team in that area. You still have to remember to call out their name so your teammates know who you are guarding," he said.

The campers split up into groups of five and started practicing. Ginny, Sophie, Aaron, Nelson, and Bart were on a team, and five other campers were on the other team. Coach Wellner led Sophie's team through choosing a spot to defend and then waiting for someone on the other team to come into their area.

A tall, African-American boy whom Sophie recognized from one of the Chicago teams came into her area, and she rolled up to him. She couldn't remember his name, but he had a number ten jersey on, so she called out, "I've got Ten!" as she blocked his path. Sophie could hear her teammates calling out the names of the people they were guarding as the other team tried to get to the hoop.

14

15

16

"Well done!" Coach Wellner said. "I like your communication! You also have to remember to listen for teammates who may need help because they have more than one person in their area. You may need to leave your own area and help them."

After their lunch break, five of the coaches lined up along the arc above the free-throw line, and Coach Frawley explained how teacup defense works.

"This is the teacup," he said. "You and your teammates line up here and wait for the other team to come down the court. When they do, you leave your spot on the line to guard them."

Five other coaches came down the court. As each of them crossed the half-court line, one of the coaches in the teacup would move from their spot to defend that person, calling out to their team to let them know who they were guarding.

"Now, let's split up into teams and start working on the teacup!" Coach Frawley called.

17

18

The campers broke into teams of five again and used small areas of the basketball court to practice. Sophie and her team lined up in a teacup formation with Sophie in the middle. Five other players came toward them. The first player came down on the right, which was closest to Ginny, so she guarded them. The next player came down on the left, which is where Aaron was, so he guarded them. Finally, the last player from the other team came down, and Sophie blocked them with her chair.

Coach Cho said, "That's right! Good formation. Good job breaking off as the other players came down. Once you have someone to guard, you stick with them as long as they're in your area unless one of your teammates needs help."

19

Each day of camp was pretty much the same. Breakfast was followed by a few hours of practice and then lunch. After lunch, there was afternoon practice, followed by dinner. There would be an evening practice after that, and then the campers got to relax. Sophie was learning so much!

20

By the last day of camp, Sophie was feeling much more confident in her basketball skills. With her new chair, she could keep up with most of the bigger kids. And with her new defensive knowledge, she knew she could stop anyone from scoring.

21

During their last practice, the campers were split up into two teams, and they scrimmaged against each other. Sophie's team started off pretty slow. By the time Coach Frawley put Sophie in the game, her team was down by ten points with only five minutes left.

The other team had the ball, so Sophie's team got into teacup formation. The players came down the court one by one, and Sophie's teammates left the teacup to guard them. The last one down the court was a tall, skinny girl whom Sophie recognized from one of the Chicago teams. Her name was Jade, and she had the ball.

"I've got Jade!" Sophie cried, pulling her chair up to Jade's. Jade stopped, dribbled once, and moved to the left. Sophie moved with her, putting the bar on the front of her chair right against Jade's chair. She moved to the right, and Sophie moved with her. Jade backed up, and Sophie followed her. Jade dribbled again, looking frustrated, and yelled, "Will someone get this little girl off of me?!" Sophie chuckled. This "little girl" wasn't going anywhere! Jade passed the ball to a boy on her team and tried to get around Sophie, who stopped her.

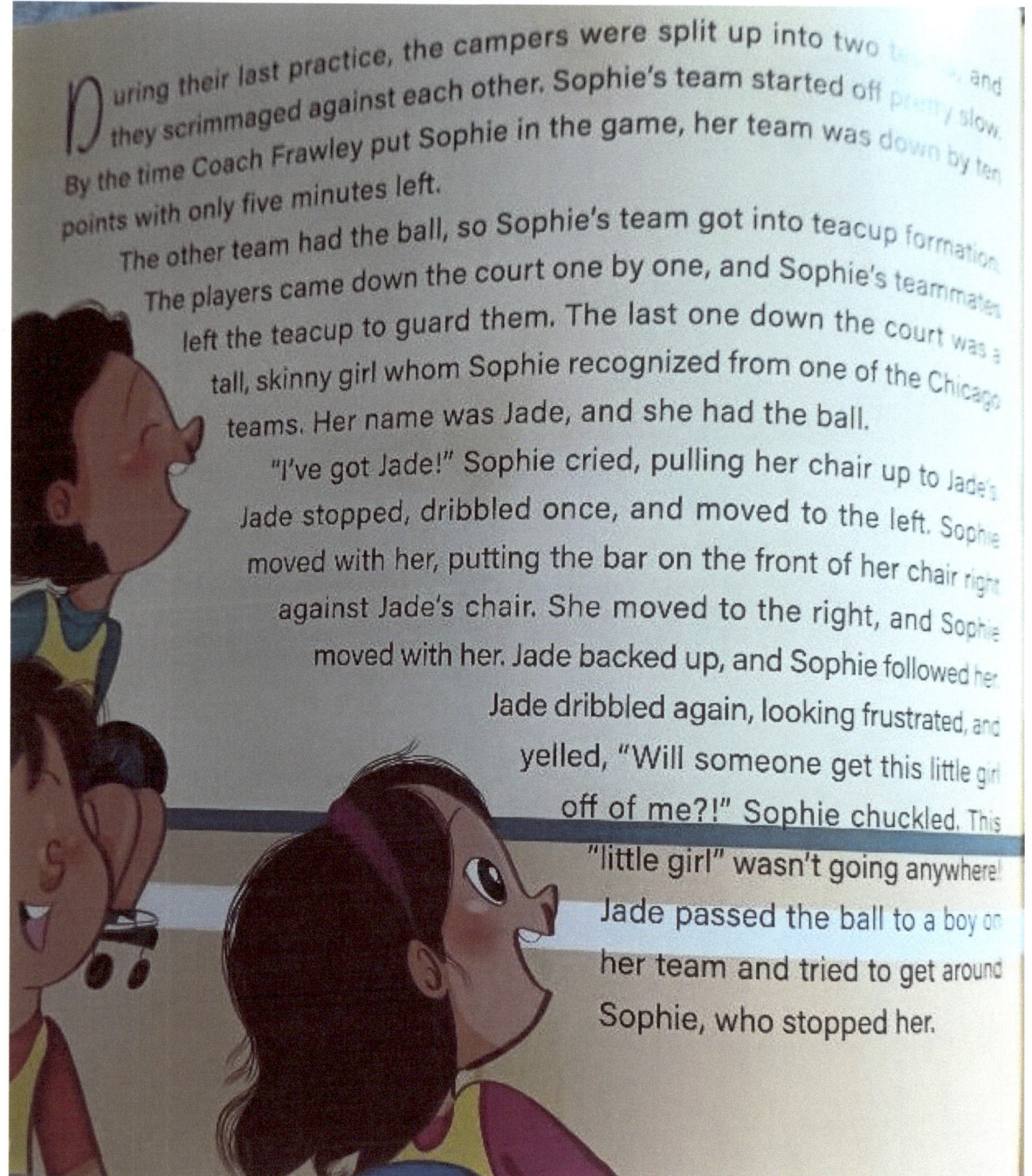

22

The boy with the ball tried to take a shot, but Aaron blocked him and grabbed the ball. Sophie took off down the court with Aaron and Ginny right behind her.

Aaron passed Sophie the ball as she got closer to the basket.

No one was guarding her! She aimed the ball and took a shot. She heard a swish as the ball flew through the net.

23

After practice, the campers packed their bags to go home. Sophie's parents arrived in their station wagon, and it was time to leave. She gave Ginny a big hug and told her she'd see her soon. Basketball season was just two months away! With her new chair and the new basketball skills she had learned at camp, Sophie knew that her second season would be even better than her first.

ABOUT THE AUTHOR

Sarah Fischer Pointer is a licensed attorney in Florida and enjoys writing children's books in her free time. Originally from Dixon, Illinois, she currently lives in Southwest Florida with her husband and their two cats. Her favorite sport is wheelchair basketball, which she played from 1996-2005 through the Blaze Sports Foundation and the Rockford Park District. Although she no longer plays basketball, she still enjoys watching it and will always consider herself a Rockford Chariot.

www.ingramcontent.com/pod-product-compliance
Lightning Source LLC
LaVergne TN
LVHW070439070526
838199LV00036B/668